Make and Play

Spies

Written by
Hazel Songhurst

Devised by
Robin Wright

Illustrated by
Dave McTaggart

zigzag

CONTENTS

This book was created by
Zigzag Publishing Ltd
5 High Street, Cuckfield
Sussex RH17 5EN, England

Edited by Nicola Wright
Designed by Chris Leishman
Photographs by Tony Potter

Colour separations by RCS Graphics Ltd, Leeds
Printed by Proost, Belgium

First published in Canada in 1993
by Zigzag Publishing Ltd
Copyright © Zigzag Publishing Ltd

10 9 8 7 6 5 4 3 2 1

ISBN 1 874647 23 2

ABOUT THIS BOOK

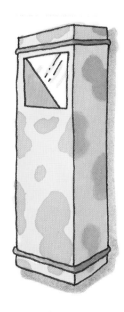

Spies are sent on dangerous secret missions. They must find out vital information, pass on important messages, stay in contact with their fellow agents, and keep an eye on the enemy, too.

This book shows you, step-by-step, how to play at being a spy and how to make the spy equipment for your mission. There are lots of ideas for disguises and a periscope to make so you can spy around corners and over walls!

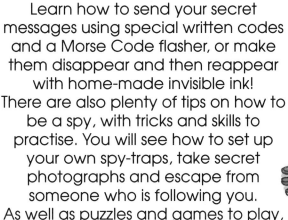

Learn how to send your secret messages using special written codes and a Morse Code flasher, or make them disappear and then reappear with home-made invisible ink!

There are also plenty of tips on how to be a spy, with tricks and skills to practise. You will see how to set up your own spy-traps, take secret photographs and escape from someone who is following you.

As well as puzzles and games to play, you will also find information about real-life spies and their spying techniques.

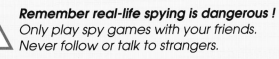

⚠️ **Remember real-life spying is dangerous !**
Only play spy games with your friends.
Never follow or talk to strangers.

WHAT YOU NEED

On these pages you can see the things
you need to make a complete spy kit and to play
the games in the book.

Silver foil

Cotton wool

Wool

Drinking straws

Face paints

Felt-tip pens

Glue

Thread

4.5v battery

Craft knife

Pencil

Crayons

Ruler

Biro

Scissors

Coloured
powder

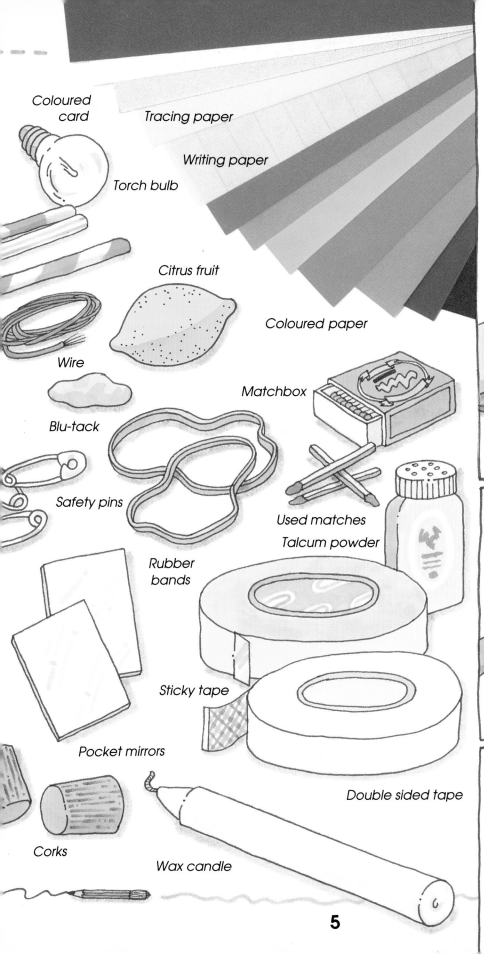

Coloured card

Tracing paper

Writing paper

Torch bulb

Citrus fruit

Coloured paper

Wire

Blu-tack

Matchbox

Safety pins

Used matches

Talcum powder

Rubber bands

Sticky tape

Pocket mirrors

Double sided tape

Corks

Wax candle

Using a craft knife

For safety, always tilt the cutting edge of the blade away from you and cut past your body. Place what you are cutting on a workboard, or a thick piece of cardboard.

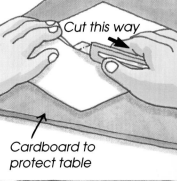

Cut this way

Cardboard to protect table

Scoring

Run the point of an empty biro firmly along lines you want to fold.

Press down hard

REMEMBER

Anything sharp or hot can harm you. When you see this danger sign, ask an adult to help you.

5

DISGUISES

A spy must not be recognized. Here are some ways to change how you look. You could think up a code name, too.

You could add a band of paper for hiding secret messages in.

Make sure your spy hat has a wide brim to hide your face.

False beards and moustaches are easy to make.

Coats with high collars help hide your face.

False beard

1 Cut a crescent shape out of brown, black,or grey material or paper to fit your face.

2 Glue on strands of black, brown or grey wool, fake fur or cotton wool.

3 Tape or glue rubber bands or loops of string to the ends of the beard and place over your ears.

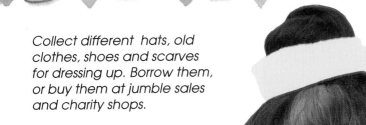

Collect different hats, old clothes, shoes and scarves for dressing up. Borrow them, or buy them at jumble sales and charity shops.

Talcum powder rubbed into your hair will make it grey if you are dark or white if you are fair.

Use face paints or make-up to draw on freckles, lines or wrinkles.

Change your hairstyle or wear a wig.

Wear sunglasses or the frames of old glasses.

False moustache and eyebrows

1 Draw a moustache and eyebrows on a piece of paper. Cut them out.

2 Glue on wool, fake fur or cotton wool. Or cut slits into the paper to make it look bushy.

3 Fix them onto your face with double-sided sticky tape.

CODES

A good way to pass on secret information is to write it in a code. Even if your message falls into enemy hands, it will stay a secret!

Line and dot code

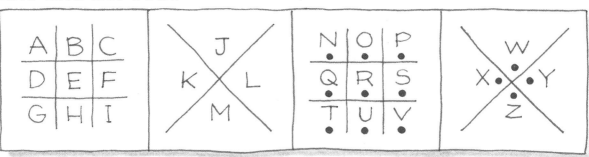

1 Copy these grids onto paper or card. Your friend will need a copy too, to decode your message.

2 You could copy each grid onto a separate piece of card and tape them together so they can be easily folded to carry in your pocket.

3 Look at the lines and dots on the grids. Instead of writing a letter of the alphabet, just use the lines and dots around it. So, A is ⌐, D is ⊐, and W is ∀.

Can you work out what this message is?

You could keep your codes hidden in a small matchbox or tin.

Window code

A simple way of sending short messages up to 20 letters in length.

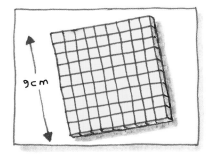

1 Cut out a square of paper or card, 9cm by 9cm. Rule lines across and down it at 1cm intervals.

2 Use a craft knife to cut out small squares - the same number as there are letters in your message.

3 Place the square on a piece of blank paper. Write your message, one letter in each hole, reading across and down.

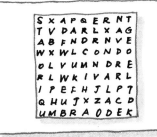

4 Remove the square and fill in the blank spaces on the paper with any letters so your message is hidden.

5 When the square is put back over the letters, the message stands out clearly.

6 Pass the cut-out square to your contact, or make an identical square for them.

Hidden letters

You can hide a secret message in a letter. For example, you could use the first and last letter in each sentence to spell it out. Or you could use the first or last words of each sentence.

Can you find the message in this letter?

It will take some practice to make the letter sound natural.

Meet Sarah at school after seeing me. Joe's friend Nic likes going to the café. 5 o'clock is the best time for swimming tonight.

HIDDEN MESSAGES

Messages must be properly hidden or they may be found by enemy spies. Here are some ideas for hiding places.

Inside your hat (or tuck it in the hat band)

In a chewing-gum pack (offer your contact a stick of gum)

Rolled up in an umbrella (say goodbye to your contact and take his or her identical umbrella)

Inside a book ('accidentally' leave it behind on a bench for your contact to pick up)

In a newspaper ('throw away' the newspaper in a litter-bin)

Spying on spies!

Arrange to meet your contact and pass on the message or leave it in a dead-letter box - a hiding place such as a hollow tree or a litter bin.

How many hiding places can you see in the picture?

In your shoe (while pretending to tie your shoe lace, slip the message from your shoe under a stone)

Make a secret badge

Put a secret message inside!

1 Cut out two card circles the same size. Glue a 3mm-wide strip of card around the edge of one circle.

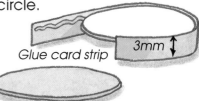

Glue card strip   3mm

2 Draw and cut out shapes. Glue them to the front of the same circle. Attach the other circle to the back with a piece of sticky tape. The front of the badge should lift off like a lid.

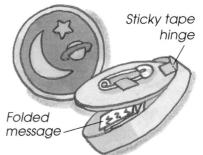

Sticky tape hinge

Folded message

3 Tape a safety pin to the back. Place your message inside, close up the badge and pin it on.

STUN GAME

Real spies are constantly in danger of being discovered and captured by the enemy. They must guard against spycatchers!

Stun dart game

Play this game with a friend and stun the enemy spies.

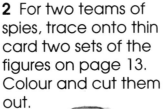

You need:
Corks
Blu-tack
Used matches
Glue
Drinking straws

DO NOT FIRE DARTS AT PEOPLE

Make 6 stun darts each.

1 To make a stun dart, stick a small piece of Blu-tack on the end of a used matchstick. Roll it between your fingers so that it fits inside the straw. Blow down the straw to fire the dart.

2 For two teams of spies, trace onto thin card two sets of the figures on page 13. Colour and cut them out.

How to play

1 Each player is a spycatcher who must try to stun the spies in the enemy team by knocking them over.

2 Arrange the two teams of spies at opposite ends of a table.

3 Take it in turns to shoot at each other's spies. To stun a spy, you must knock it over.

4 When you have used all your darts, add up the numbers on the backs of the spies you have stunned to find your scores. The person with the highest score is the winner.

3 Draw a number on the back of each figure. See the scoring details opposite for which numbers to use.

4 Cut a slot in the top of the corks and glue a figure in each one.

Scoring

Each team is led by one Master Spy, worth 10 points.

Each team has a Double-Agent worth 5 points. If you hit the Double-Agent, you double your total score.

The rest of your spies should be numbered 1, 2, 3 and 4.

Both players choose a new Mole at the start of each game. Write down the number of yours, but keep it a secret until the end of the game.

If your opponent shoots your Mole he or she loses the number of points on the Mole's back.

Trace these figures.

SECRET WRITING

H   U   Z   L   E

W

J

Q

C

N

K

G

S

Z

Fool your enemies by writing invisible messages. Make sure your friends know how to make them reappear.

Invisible ink

Orange, lemon and grapefruit juices make the best inks. You could also try potato juice, onion juice or milk.

You could sharpen the matchstick in a pencil sharpener.

Store the juice in a clean, empty jar or bottle with a lid.

1 Cut the fruit in half and squeeze out the juice. An egg cup makes a good container.

2 Dip a used matchstick into the juice and use it to write a message.

3 When the juice dries, the writing will have vanished.

ASK AN ADULT TO HELP

Remember to add a clue to show there is an invisible message.

Write your message in between the lines of an ordinary letter.

The message reappears in clear, brown writing.

4 To read the message, heat the paper on the top shelf of a cool oven - Gas Mark 2, 300°F or 150°C. Check it every few minutes so it doesn't get too hot.

ty

ou had a good

the seaside with

ed. Did you buy

k for me and

m says she

Dear Aunty

Meet me at the

I hope you had

Magic pencil

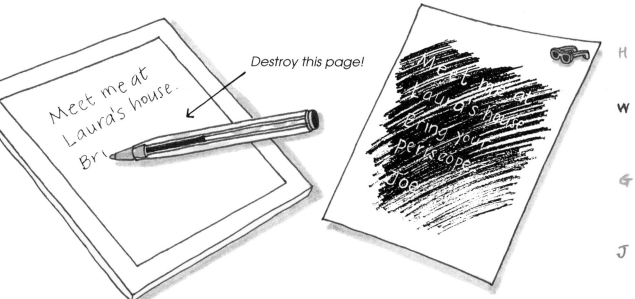

Destroy this page!

1 Write a message with a pencil or biro on a notepad. Press hard so it leaves marks on the next page.

2 The outlines should show up faintly on the next page.

3 To read the message, scribble gently all over the page with a pencil. The writing will show up white.

Wax writing

1 Wax some paper by rubbing it with a candle or crayon. Lay the waxed side on plain paper.

2 Press hard when writing your secret message so that it prints in wax marks on the plain paper.

3 To read the message, sprinkle coloured powder over it. The powder will stick to the message but slide off the rest of the paper.

For coloured powder you could use instant powdered coffee, coloured chalk scrapings or dry powder paint.

B   F   L   T

LOOKING AND LISTENING

Real spies use special equipment to help them listen secretly to conversations, and to keep a hidden watch on people. You can make your own 'spywatch' equipment.

Bugs

A bug has a tiny microphone inside it. If it is hidden in a room, a spy outside can overhear conversations.

A plastic bottle cap covered with foil makes a realistic-looking bug.

You could disguise your bugs by making them look like insects or sweets.

Fill your bug with Blu-tack so that it sticks easily to surfaces. Or tape a little magnet to it for sticking on metal surfaces.

Spider bug - pipecleaner legs

Liquorice bug

Sweet bug - disguised in an old sweet wrapper

Flower bug - paper petals

Ladybird bug - paper spotted wings

Fly bug - plastic wings

Hiding place

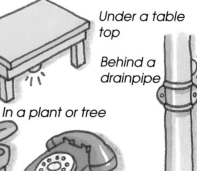

Under a table top

Behind a drainpipe

In a plant or tree

Under a phone

Bugged !

1 Throw a die. The player who scores highest hides the bugs.

2 The other players leave the room and count to 100.

3 The players return to the room and look for the bugs. Set a time limit - perhaps 5 minutes.

4 The player who finds the most bugs hides them in the next round.

Periscope

Use a periscope for looking around corners, or for spying over a wall or fence.

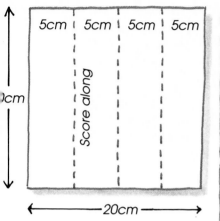

5cm | 5cm | 5cm | 5cm

Score along

0cm

←——— 20cm ———→

You need :

Piece of cardboard
20cm x 60cm, or an
empty silver foil or
cling film box
2 pocket mirrors
Scissors
Rubber bands
Pencil and ruler

4 Bend the cardboard round to make a tube. Fasten rubber bands round each end. Place a mirror at each end, using the diagonal lines you drew as a guide.

1 Draw three lines 5cm apart along the card, as shown. Score along the lines so you can bend the cardboard.

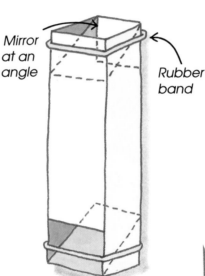

Mirror at an angle

Rubber band

You could add paper leaves to camouflage your periscope.

2 Draw two lines across, 6cm from the top and bottom. Cut out the squares shown in the drawing below.

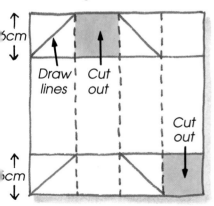

6cm

Draw lines | Cut out

Cut out

6cm

3 Draw lines diagonally across the four squares shown in the diagram.

Adjust the angle of the mirrors until when you hold the periscope just above a wall or fence, you can see something reflected from the top mirror into the bottom mirror.

If the mirrors drop out, fasten the rubber bands more tightly.

17

SENDING SIGNALS

In a dangerous situation, it may be best to signal an urgent message. Make a Morse Code flasher and send for help fast !

Morse flasher

You need :

4.5 volt battery with flat metal connecting strips
Torch bulb
Strip of cardboard folded in two
Matchbox
2 x 20cm-long wires
1 x 10mm-long wires
Blu-tack, sticky tape, foil

1 Bare about 4cm of the ends of the wires.

2 Wrap the ends of the 20cm-long wires round the connecting strips of the battery. Fasten with tape.

3 Wrap the other end of one of the longer wires round the bulb. Tape the end of the shorter wire to the base of the bulb. Secure with tape or Blu-tack.

4 Wrap a piece of foil round the free end of the other long wire. Stick it to the card strip with Blu-tack.

5 Wrap foil round the free end of the short wire and stick it to the other end of the card strip.

6 Press the folded card strip down so the pieces of foil touch. The bulb will light up.

Cut holes in the ends of a matchbox for the bulb and wires to go through.

If the bulb doesn't light, make sure all the connections are firmly fixed.

How to send a Morse Code message

This is the Morse Code. Each letter of the alphabet is a different arrangement of dots and dashes. To flash your Morse Code message, make short flashes for dots and long ones for dashes.

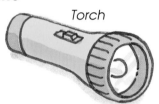

● Short flash

▬ Long flash

A	B	C	D	E	F
G	H	I	J	K	L
M	N	O	P	Q	R
S	T	U	V	W	X
Y	Z				

Make your own signals

Flash messages with a mirror or a torch: two flashes for danger, three for all clear.

Torch

Mirror

Body language

Make up signals: for example, rubbing your nose could mean 'Meet me later.'

Scratching your ear - 'I'll telephone you later.'

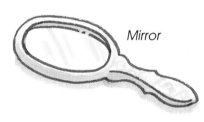
Rubbing your eyes - 'Be careful, you're being watched.'

Scratching your head - 'Don't do anything.'

Hands behind back - 'I can't pass a message now.'

One hand in pocket - 'Yes.'

Two hands in pockets - 'No.'

TRICKS AND SKILLS

To outwit the enemy, a clever spy must know all kinds of tricks and skills. Here are some important ones.

Spy-traps

How do you know if an enemy agent has got into your room? Here are some ways to make it spy-proof.

If someone opens the door the hair will break!

If someone comes in, the box will fall.

Tape the thread low down.

Glue a hair across a door or drawer. When you return, check to see if it is still there.

Tape thread onto a small open box. Fill it with rice or flour. Tape the other end to the door. Balance the box on the door frame.

Tape a thin cotton thread across a door opening or between two walls. It will fall down if someone walks through it.

Mark the position of furniture and objects in your room with chalk marks. Then you will be able to tell if anything has been moved.

Sprinkle talcum powder on the floor. An intruder's footprints will show up clearly.

Remember to ask an adult's permission before setting any of these spy traps

Shake off a tail

Try these tricks with a friend tailing (following) you.

Carry a quick disguise. Dash into a doorway and walk out looking different.

Head for a crowd. It will keep you hidden from view.

Suddenly turn and face your 'tail'. If he or she turns and walks away, run down a side street.

Keep changing direction. Take a zig-zag route or go the longest way round.

Turn a corner, sit down on a bench and hide your face in a newspaper until your 'tail' has passed.

Make a dummy

If you think you are being watched by someone outside the house, make a dummy by putting your clothes around pillows and propping them up. Seat it near a window. Slip out of the back door and leave your enemy to keep an eye on it!

SPYWATCH

Governments send up satellites and planes into the sky to take photographs to find out information about other countries.

Hidden camera

A camera can be a very useful part of a spy's equipment for collecting important evidence. You may have your own camera. If not, you could borrow one or buy one of the cheap 'throwaway' cameras now available.

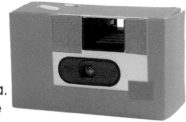

There are lots of ways you can hide your camera and yourself so that no-one knows you are taking photographs.

Wind down the car window as you drive past.

Hide your camera under your coat until the last moment.

Keep your camera hidden in a bag.

Hide yourself behind a newspaper and cut a small hole in it for your camera lens to peep through.

Pretend to be taking a photo in another direction, then swing round.

Hide behind or in a tree!

Simon Spyman's photos

Here is a photo taken by Simon Spyman. See if you can spot any suspicious goings-on.

Spy plane

Make model spy planes with your friends and fly them over each other's territory.

You need :
Pencil
Used matchsticks
Rubber bands

Coloured card
Coloured paper
Glue
Scissors

Start at the corner

Glue down edge

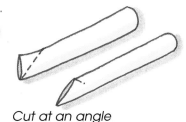

Cut at an angle

1 Cut out a triangle with sides the same length as your pencil. Roll it round the pencil to make the body of the plane.

2 Glue the edge down and slide the pencil out.

3 Squeeze and glue one end down. Cut it at an angle to make the nose of the plane.

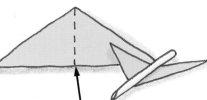

Score and bend up

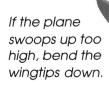

About 4cm slit

Glue matchstick at an angle

4 Use a triangle of card for the wings. Score and bend along the middle and across the wingtips. Glue to the body.

5 Cut out a tail fin. Make a slit at the tail end of the body, slide the tail fin in and glue.

6 Make a hole under the nose and glue in a matchstick at an angle.

Flying the plane

Hook a rubber band over the matchstick. Pull the tail fin back in one hand and pull the elastic band in front with the other. Let go of the plane and watch it fly !

If the plane swoops up too high, bend the wingtips down.

If the plane dives, bend the wingtips up more.

Spy plane game

Lay large squares of different coloured paper on the ground for territories. If you fly your plane over another person's territory, win 5 points. If you land on their territory, win 10 points.

SPY MAZE

Spy

The blue-coated spy in the basement of the castle has the secret plans. Can you help him find a way through the maze and out of the castle before the yellow-coated spycatchers close in on him?

SPY FACTS

Devices and gadgets

Here are some of the hi-tec devices and gadgets that spies use today. Many of them are used for spying on business meetings (called industrial espionage).

Pen transmitter (bug) : records conversations over 100 metres away.

Telephone transmitter (bug): a tiny recording device which is hidden in the telephone and starts recording both sides of the conversation as soon as someone speaks.

Digital voice changer: a microphone that fits over the mouthpiece of a telephone and disguises voices by making men's voices sound like women's, and women's sound like men's.

Earspy: a tiny electronic device that fits in the ear and receives messages from a contact. A miniature microphone (hidden under a jacket lapel or tie) enables the spy to reply.

Video briefcase: a special briefcase containing a miniature video camera with a lens the size of a pinhole. It can be turned on by changing the briefcase's combination lock.

'Antenna' camera: it looks like an ordinary car aerial, but hidden inside is a tiny camera lens. The rest of the camera is hidden under the bodywork.

Bug detector: an electronic 'sweeping' device that detects and locates bugs.

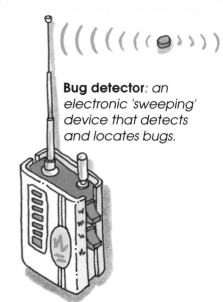

Night vision goggles: enable you to see clearly in the dark.

Laser bugging: a laser beam is aimed at a window and picks up conversations by analyzing the minute vibrations of the glass made by the sound of voices.

Famous spy stories

In 500 BC, a greek spy went on a long journey to deliver a message. It was perfectly hidden – tattooed on his head! It could be read only when his hair was shaved off.

Lord Baden-Powell, founder of the boy scout movement, spent months learning about butterflies so he could go on an army mission disguised as a butterfly collector. He sketched details of enemy weapons into the patterns of butterfly wings he was drawing.

Charles Eon de Beaumont was a French spy who lived in the eighteenth century. He was sent on a mission to a Russian court disguised as a woman. He was so successful that the Russian empress actually made him her maid of honour.

Mata Hari, a Dutch woman, was a famous spy during World War 1. Her real name was Gertrud Zelle. She became a dancer in Paris, and worked for both the German and French Secret Services. She was not a very good spy and was not loyal to either side. Eventually she was arrested by the French and shot by firing squad.

Worldwide intelligence services

Most countries have an intelligence service. Their job is usually to collect information secretly about what is happening in other countries. Here are a few of them:

CIA	USA's Central Intelligence Agency
FBI	USA's spy-catching organization
MI6	Britain's international Secret Service
MI5	Britain's mainland Secret Service, working closely with the Special Branch of the police force.
KGB	Secret Service of the former Soviet Union
ASIO	Australian Secret Intelligence Organization
BOSS	South Africa's intelligence service
CESID	Spain's intelligence service
CSIS	Canadian Security Intelligence Service

SPY WORDS

Bug A tiny hidden listening device.

Burnt A word used to describe a spy who has been discovered by the enemy.

Cobbler A forger of passports.

Code-name The name a spy is known by.

Contact A member of a spy ring or group.

Dead-letter box A place to hide messages.

Decode To work out a coded message.

Double-agent A spy working for two countries at the same time.

Drop To leave a message for another spy.

Encode To put a message into code.

Espionage Another word for spying.

Fix To blackmail.

Going private To leave the Secret Service.

Hospital Prison.

Intelligence Information.

Master spy The head of a spy ring.

Mole A spy who joins the enemy to steal their secrets.

Pavement artist A spy keeping watch on a house.

Peep A spy photographer.

Piano study Radio operating.

Plant To hide something secretly, such as a bug.

Playback When a spy is caught and forced to send false information.

Plumbing Preparation for a major operation.

Safe house A hideaway.

Secret agent Another name for a spy.

Shadowing Secretly following the enemy.

Shoe A false passport.

Spycatcher A spy who traps enemy spies.

Spy ring A team of spies.

Stroller A spy using a walkie-talkie.

Tail A spy who follows another.

Thirty-threes An emergency.

Turned agent A spy who leaves to work for the other side.

Undercover Working in disguise.

What's your twenty? Where exactly are you?

Index